T0145311

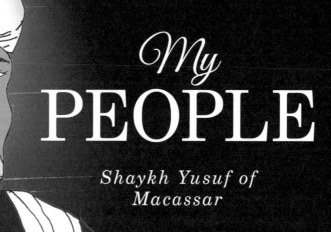

My
PEOPLE

*Shaykh Yusuf of
Macassar*

BY:

**Suraya Esau nee
Houtappel/Jabaar**

ILLUSTRATED BY:

Kothar Esau

Balboa Press books may be ordered through booksellers or by contacting:

Balboa Press
A Division of Hay House
1663 Liberty Drive
Bloomington, IN 47403
www.balboapress.com.au
1 (877) 407-4847

ISBN: 978-1-5043-1520-3 (sc)
ISBN: 978-1-5043-1521-0 (e)

Print information available on the last page.

Balboa Press rev. date: 10/12/2018

BALBOA.
PRESS
A DIVISION OF HAY HOUSE

My PEOPLE

Shaykh Yusuf of Macassar

This book is dedicated to the Cape Muslims who have gone through generations of hardship due to colonization. May this book help future generations to find their identity through knowing their history.

Once there lived a carefree boy from a noble background. Every day Yusuf would play in the fields of Macassar, near the palace where he lived. His world was all at peace.

He grew up learning the *Quran.*

When Yusuf was eighteen years old he decided to explore the world. Yusuf travelled far and wide. On his travels Yusuf went to Mecca and learned all about Islam.

One day Yusuf decided to come back to his people. He decided to teach his people about Islam. The people loved Yusuf. They called him the PIOUS one, the KIND one, the TOLERANT one and the LEARNED one. Yusuf became known as Shaykh Yusuf.

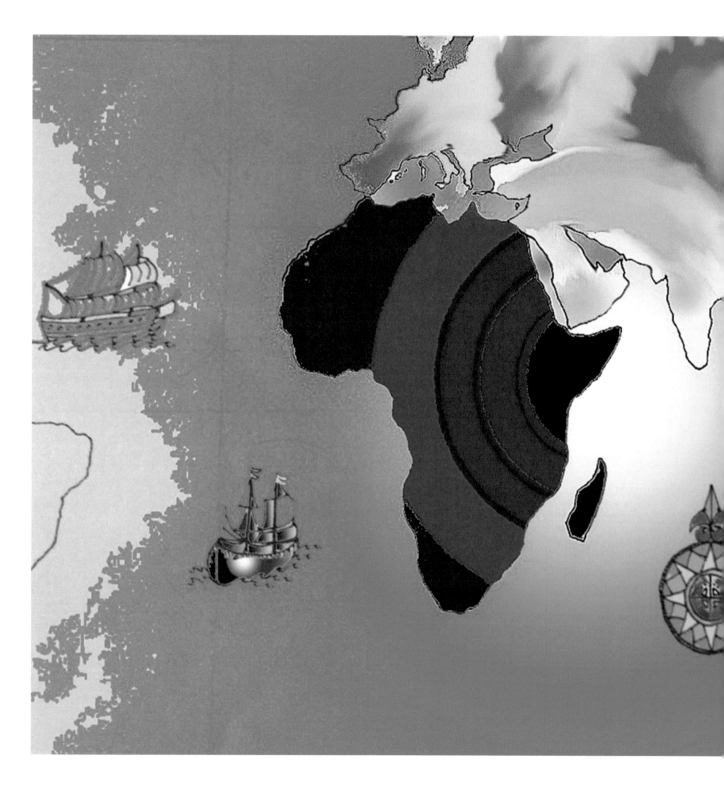

Shaykh Yusuf worked hard teaching his people about Islam and how to be kind and merciful. His people became one of the most educated at the time. They lived happily for many, many years until one day the Dutch came and took over the country.

The people ran to Shaykh Yusuf and asked him what they could do. Shaykh Yusuf knew the Dutch were strong and powerful. So he told his people to run to the hills.

However, the Dutch knew where they were going and they trapped them. Many of Shaykh Yusuf's people ran away while others died.

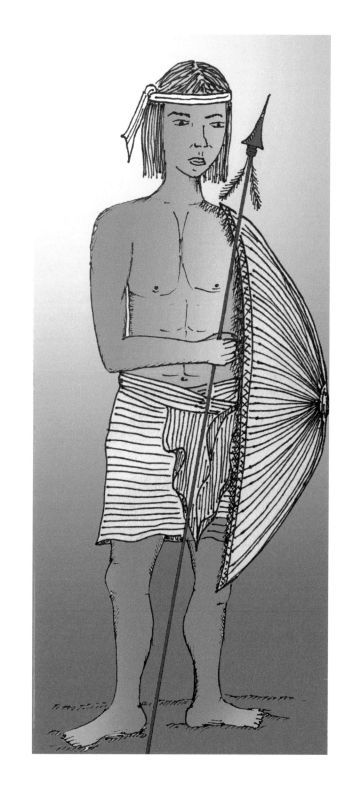

Shaykh Yusuf and some of the people hid in a small village but soon they were captured. He was taken far away from his people but Shaykh Yusuf continued to influence more people to come to Islam.

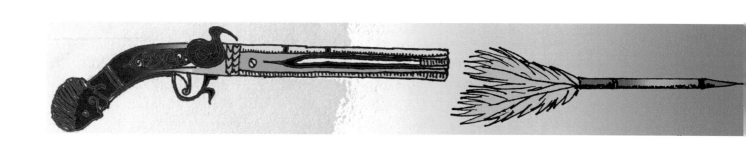

Shaykh Yusuf's people called him a hero and begged the Dutch to release him and bring him home. But they wouldn't.

Instead, Shaykh Yusuf was sent even farther away from his people. He was sent on a ship called the Voetboeg to a far, far away place, far away from his people.

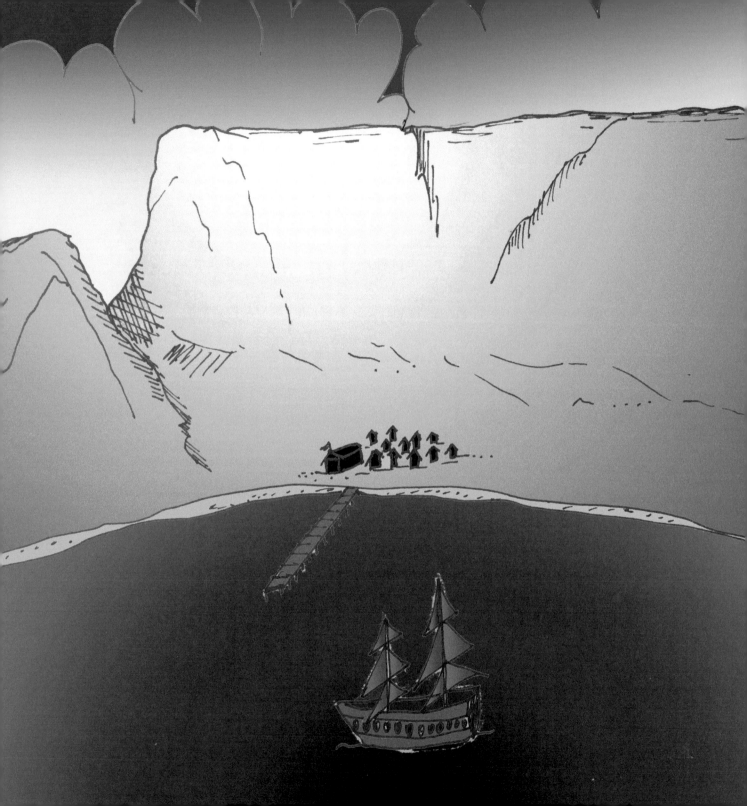

When Shaykh Yusuf was brought to the Cape of Good Hope, he had a lot of hope within himself. His hope was to spread Islam far and wide.

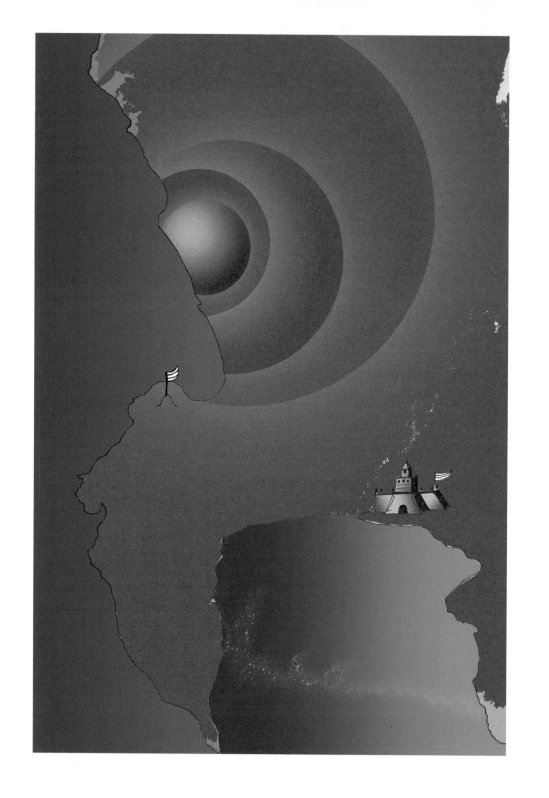

The Dutch sent him to an isolated place known as Zandvliet. But Shaykh Yusuf refused to give up. He started another community and taught them also about Islam. Again, Shaykh Yusuf became a hero and Islam started in the Cape.

After five years of establishing a new community, Shaykh Yusuf died and was buried in Zandvliet. And that's how Islam spread to Cape Town.

THE END

Printed in the United States
By Bookmasters